ENGLISH PRACTICE AND PROGRESS

VOCABULARY ACTIVITIES
(ELEMENTARY)

SUE FINNIE & DANIÈLE BOURDAIS

SCHOLASTIC

MARY GLASGOW MAGAZINES

Contents

My Family

Complete the crossword.

1 My parents' son is my …

2 My mother's mother is my …

3 My mother's brother is my …

4 I call her 'Mum'. She's my …

5 I call him 'Dad'. He's my …

6 My father's father is my …

7 My father's sister is my …

8 My parents' daughter is my …

This is Andrew. He's my

C _ _ _ _ _

Now write the letters from inside the circles above. Unscramble the letters to find out what Emily is saying.

COUSIN

Crossword answers:
1 BROTHER
2 GRANDMOTHER
3 UNCLE
4 MOTHER
5 FATHER
6 GRANDFATHER
7 AUNT
8 SISTER

Family Tree

This is Coco the Clown and his family.
Read the information and write the names to complete the family tree.

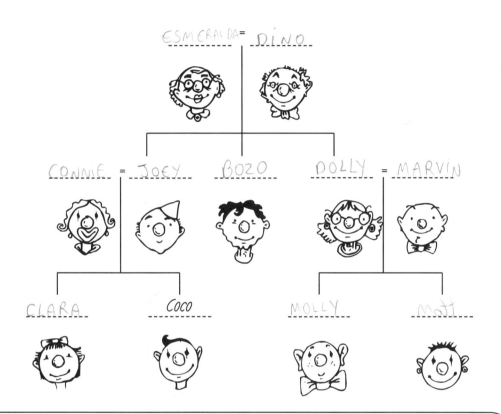

★ Coco's sister is called Clara.
★ Their mother is Connie.
★ Her husband is Joey.
★ Coco's grandfather is Joey's father. His name is Dino.

★ Dino has got two sons. One is called Bozo.
★ Coco's grandmother is Esmerelda.
★ Esmerelda has got a daughter called Dolly.

★ Dolly has got a son called Matt.
★ Marvin's wife is Dolly.
★ Coco has got a cousin called Molly.

Who is wrong?

I've got two uncles and an aunt.

I've got a wife, a son and a daughter.

I've got three children and four grandchildren.

I've got two brothers and two cousins.

Football Training

Today is football training and you've got the shirts for the youth club football team. Who gets which number? Read the sentences and write a number on each player's shirt.

(1) Player number 1 is tall and quite fat. He's got long, straight black hair. He doesn't wear glasses.

(2) Player number 2 is short and quite fat. Her hair is medium-length, dark and curly.

(3) Player number 3 has got dark hair, too. His hair is short and straight. He's short and very thin.

(4) Player number 4 is slim and quite short. She wears glasses. She's got long, curly blond hair.

(5) Player number 5 has also got blond hair. His hair is straight and medium-length. He's tall and fat and doesn't wear glasses.

(6) Player number 6 is also tall and quite fat. He's got short, blond curly hair.

(7) Player number 7 is tall and slim. She doesn't wear glasses. She's got long, straight, brown hair.

(8) Player number 8 has also got brown hair but her hair is medium-length and curly. She's tall and slim.

(9) Player number 9 is quite short and quite fat. He's got short, straight blond hair and he wears glasses.

(10) Player number 10 doesn't wear glasses. She's tall with medium-length, curly blond hair.

(11) Player number 11 has got short, black hair. She's tall and quite slim.

The referee hasn't got a number on his shirt. Draw a circle around the referee. Then write a description of him.

The Monster

Write the names of the parts of the body. Use the words in the box.

head   ear   eye   nose   mouth   chin
arm   hand   stomach   leg   foot

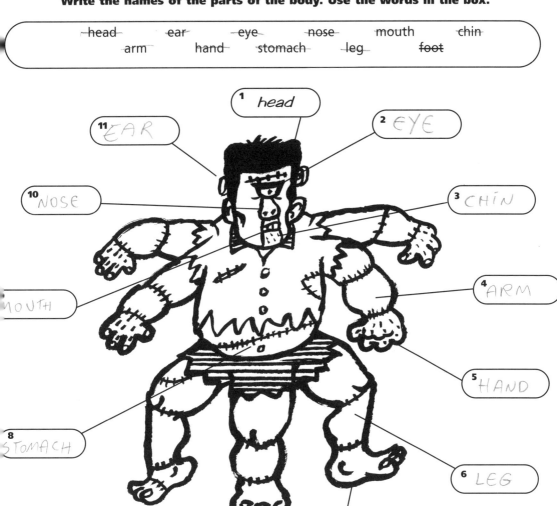

1 head
11 EAR
2 EYE
10 NOSE
3 CHIN
MOUTH
4 ARM
5 HAND
8 STOMACH
6 LEG
7 FOOT

What has the monster got? Write True or False.

He's got one eye.

True.

3 He's got three feet.

TRUE

5 He's got two chins.

FALSE

He's got two ears.

FALSE

4 He's got one nose.

TRUE

Now write five more sentences about the monster.

7

Personality Spiral

Write the adjectives in the box in the correct place on the spiral.
The first letter of each adjective is already on the spiral.

brave
clever
funny
generous
happy
honest
mad
patient
polite
rude
selfish
shy
sociable
stupid
talkative

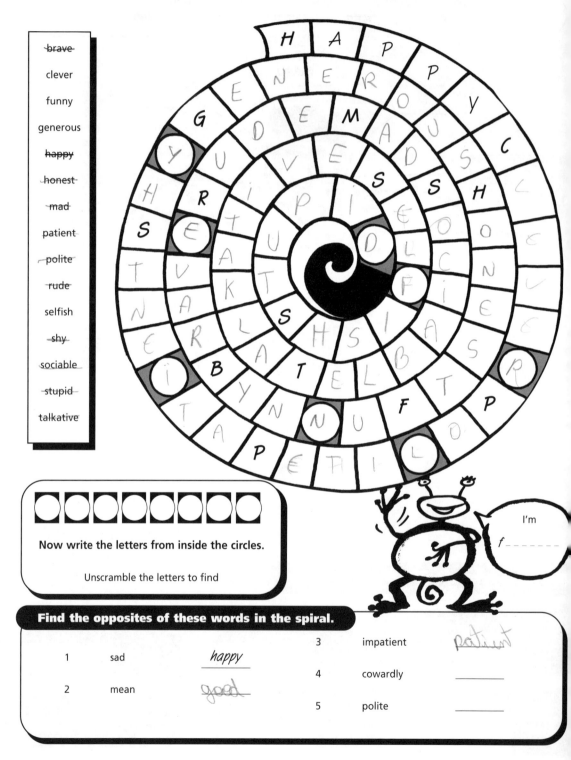

Now write the letters from inside the circles.

Unscramble the letters to find

I'm
f _ _ _ _ _ _

Find the opposites of these words in the spiral.

1	sad	*happy*	3	impatient	patient
2	mean	good	4	cowardly	_____
			5	polite	_____

How Sensitive Are You?

Complete the personality quiz.

1

There's a new boy in your class. He's very quiet. What do you think?

❋ He's shy. Perhaps he's sad.

☆ It's OK. Some people aren't very talkative.

❂ He's very rude!

3

The bus is late. How do you feel?

❂ Impatient and angry. Stupid bus!

☆ A bit impatient.

❋ Worried – perhaps there's a problem with the bus.

2

Your mother is very tired. What do you say?

❂ Don't be lazy!

❋ Let me help you! Really, I insist!

☆ Can I help you?

4

A friend finds some money in the street and she puts it in her pocket. What do you think?

❋ That's OK – she hasn't got a lot of money.

❂ She's selfish. She should give me some money!

☆ She isn't very honest – whose money is it?

5

Your neighbour's dog is ill. What do you say?

☆ Don't worry. I'm sure he'll be better soon.

❋ That's really terrible. Try to be brave.

❂ Don't be stupid, it's only a dog!

6

Which do you prefer to be?

❋ polite

☆ friendly

❂ funny

Add up your points and check your results.

POINTS

❋ = 5 points
☆ = 3 points
❂ = 1 point

12 points or less: You aren't very sensitive and sometimes you can be rude. Try to think of other people and be more thoughtful.

13 – 20 points: You're a friendly, sociable person. You're honest and quite generous. Sometimes you're sensitive, but try to think of others a bit more often.

21 – 30 points: You're polite, generous and very sensitive. You aren't selfish and you always think of others. Did you answer the questions honestly?!

How Old Are You?

Read the sentences. Tick True or False.

Balvir

I'm eleven.
My birthday's on the
19th of March.

Gina

I'm twelve.
My birthday's on
St Valentine's Day –
the 14th of February.

Lauren

I'm twelve.
My birthday's in the
summer. It's on the
2nd of August.

Anna

I'm fourteen.
My birthday is on
the 25th of June.
I love birthdays!

Danny

I'm thirteen.
My birthday's in
the winter. It's on the
19th of December.

Scott

I'm thirteen and
my birthday's on the
21st of October.

	True	False
a. Balvir is 11.	✓	☐
b. Scott is 13.	☐	☐
c. Lauren is 14.	☐	☐
d. Gina's birthday is on the 14th of February.	☐	☐
e. Anna's birthday is on the 27th of July.	☐	☐
f. Danny's birthday is in December.	☐	☐
g. Lauren's birthday is in summer.	☐	☐
h. Balvir's birthday is in autumn.	☐	☐
i. Anna's birthday is in summer.	☐	☐
j. Both boys are 13.	☐	☐
k. Two of the girls are 14.	☐	☐
l. Scott's birthday is in autumn.	☐	☐
m. St Valentine's day is in February.	☐	☐
n. Gina and Lauren are 12.	☐	☐
o. Danny's birthday is in spring.	☐	☐
p. December is in winter.	☐	☐

Colour the picture to find out how old Lauren's cat is.

 If the statement is true, colour the section of the picture black.

 If the statement is false, leave the section white.

Lauren's cat is _____

Inventions

Do you know the origin of these inventions?

Look at the pictures and read the sentences. Choose the correct nationality.

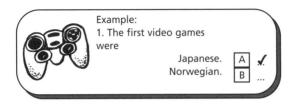

Example:
1. The first video games were

Japanese. A ✔
Norwegian. B ...

2. The first guitar was

Spanish. M ✔
Scottish. E ...

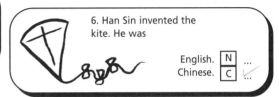

6. Han Sin invented the kite. He was

English. N ...
Chinese. C ✔

3. The first hamburgers were

German. E ...
American. B ✔

7. The man who made the first sandwich was

English. A ✔
French. H ...

4. The company that first produced the mini-disc in 1992 was

Indian. I ...
Japanese. R ✔

8. Cesare Bertana made the first postcard in 1865. Bertana was

Italian. N ✔
Portuguese. L ...

5. The man who invented Lego® bricks was

Russian. E ...
Danish. I ✔

Write the letters of the eight correct answers to finish the nationality word that completes this sentence.

The first jukeboxes were

A M B R I C A N
1 2 3 4 5 6 7 8

Puzzle It Out!

**These kids at the fair have each won a giant teddy bear.
Read the clues and fill in the names on the board.**

- One girl feels happy, but it's not Anna.
- The girl called Carly feels thirsty.
- The boy called Daniel feels sad.
- Robbie feels sick.
- Elena doesn't feel tired.
- Simon feels hungry.

The first letters of the names spell
out how Luke feels!

Luke feels S C A R E D !

Feeling ill

What's wrong with the monster?
Cross out the words in the grid and write them next to each picture.

Oh, doctor!
I have a terrible ...

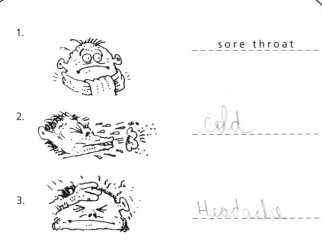

1. _ _ _ _ sore throat _ _ _ _

2. _ _ cold _ _

3. _ Headache _ _ _

4. _ Tooth Ache _ _

5. _ stomach Ache _

6. _ ear ache _ _

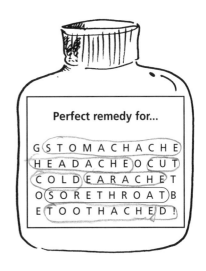

Perfect remedy for...

```
G S T O M A C H A C H E
H E A D A C H E O C U T
C O L D E A R A C H E T
O S O R E T H R O A T B
E T O O T H A C H E D !
```

**Use the other letters to find
out what the doctor says!**

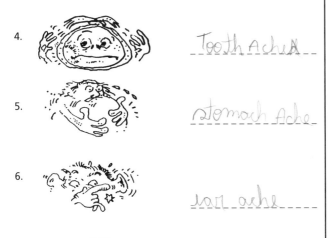

7. _ cut _

In My Opinion...

What do these people think about these hobbies?
Match each sentence to the correct picture.

Fishing is relaxing.   Reading is interesting.   Shopping is great fun.   Parachuting is exciting.

Parachuting is frightening.   Shopping is irritating.   Fishing is boring.   Reading is OK.

1. _____!

2. _____!

3. _____!

4. _____!

5. _____!

6. _____!

7. _____!

8. _____!

Dates for your Calendar

Read what Ranjit says about these special days and write them on the calendar.

JANUARY	FEBRUARY	MARCH
APRIL	MAY	JUNE
JULY	AUGUST *3rd Ranjit's Birthday*	SEPTEMBER
OCTOBER	NOVEMBER	DECEMBER

My birthday: It's on the 3rd of the month before September. This year I am 14.
Christmas Day: It's on the 25th of the last month of the year. We send cards and get presents.
Bonfire Night: It's on the 5th of the month before December. In the park, there is a bonfire and fireworks.
Diwali: It's the Hindu festival of light. This year, it's the month before November. We have a big party.
New Year's Day: It's the first day of the first month of the year. I stay up very late the night before.
Valentine's Day: It's the 14th of the month after January. I'm going to send a card to a girl I like.
Exams start: At school my exams start on the 10th of the month after April. Oh no!
Summer holidays start: School finishes on 24th of the month before August. Yes!!!
Mother's Day: I'm going to send my mum a card in the month before April.
Father's Day: I'm going to send my dad a card in the month after May.

Add some more important dates to the calendar (Easter, Spring holiday, Halloween, your birthday, family and friends' birthdays, etc.).

Numbers Picture

How many of the things in the list can you find?

monkeys — *There are*
three monkeys

sea lions — ----------------

zoo-keepers — ----------------

elephants — ----------------

clouds — ----------------

trees — ----------------

lions — ----------------

dustbins — ----------------

butterflies — ----------------

birds — ----------------

children — ----------------

On the Washing Line

Unscramble the letters and write the names of the clothes.

HRSIT

-SITHRT

WITHE RSATS

KRITS

RUOTSRES

SENJA

DESRS

CKOSS

1. s h i r (t)
2. _ - _ _ _ (O) _
3. s w e (a) t s h i r t
4. _ _ (O) _ _
5. _ _ _ (O) _
6. _ _ _ _ (O) _
7. _ (O) _ _ _
8. _ _ _ _ (O) _

Now write the letters from inside the circles to find out what Kevin is wearing on his feet.

Kevin is wearing (t) _ _ _ _ _ _ _ _

Now read the sentences and colour in the clothes.

The jeans are blue.   The shirt is pink.   The sweatshirt is yellow.
The T-shirt is black.   The dress is purple.   The trousers are brown.
          The socks are blue and white.   The skirt is red.

Hide and Seek

Read the descriptions. Who's hiding behind the tree?
Write the names next to the people.

• Peter is wearing a white T-shirt, a bomber jacket, black trousers and black shoes.

• Paul is wearing a cap, a white shirt, a jumper, jeans and trainers.

• Laura is wearing a white skirt, a jumper and white shoes.

• Sophie is wearing a white shirt, a grey skirt, a leather jacket and sandals.

Now draw the other two people hidin behind the second tree.

Eurocolours

Colour by numbers.
Colour these fifteen European flags

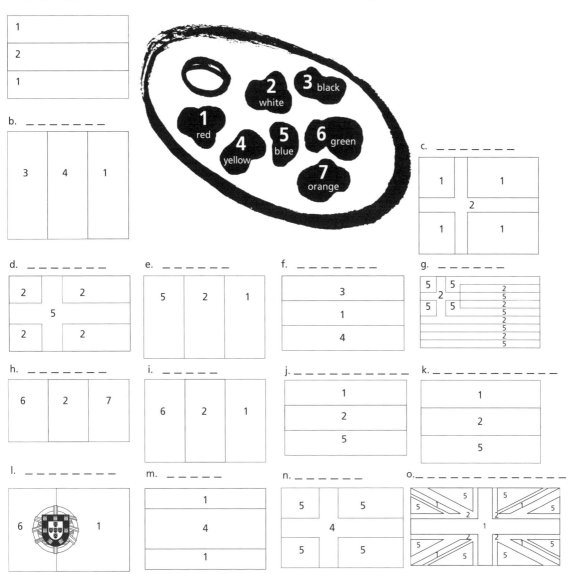

a. *Austria*

b. _ _ _ _ _ _ _

c. _ _ _ _ _ _ _

d. _ _ _ _ _ _ _

e. _ _ _ _ _ _

f. _ _ _ _ _ _

g. _ _ _ _ _ _

h. _ _ _ _ _ _

i. _ _ _ _ _

j. _ _ _ _ _ _ _ _

k. _ _ _ _ _ _ _ _ _ _

l. _ _ _ _ _ _ _

m. _ _ _ _ _ _

n. _ _ _ _ _ _

o. _ _ _ _ _ _ _ _ _ _ _ _ _ _

Now write the name of each country. Use the words in the box.

Netherlands   Belgium   United Kingdom   ~~Austria~~   Finland
Luxembourg Ireland   Germany   Denmark   Greece   Italy
Portugal   France   Sweden   Spain

Fruity Fun!

Find the fruit in the grid.
Write the correct name under each fruit.

orange
....

....

O	P	D	O	Y	G	O	C
R	U	E	L	I	R	K	H
A	P	E	A	S	A	T	E
N	K	L	R	R	P	A	R
G	I	W	U	B	E	E	R
E	W	R	R	M	S	I	I
E	I	A	P	P	L	E	E
B	A	N	A	N	A	S	S

....

....

....

....

....

....

Use the other letters in the grid to write the worm's question.

_ _   _ _ _ _   _ _ _ _ _

_ _ _ _ _ _ _ _ _ _ _ _ _?

What is your favourite fruit?

_____

Picnic Crossword

Look at Nicky's picnic. Fill in the grid.

Nicky forgot her favourite food. Rearrange the letters in the grey squares to find out what it is.

Which Shop?

**Move around the hexagons in the correct order to find the names of the shops.
Write the names on the shops.**

Health Quiz

**How healthy are you? To complete the quiz, look at the phrases below
and write them next to the correct picture.**

1. ~~eat fruit and vegetables~~
2. walk to school
3. eat cakes and biscuits
4. smoke
5. drink fizzy drinks
6. watch TV
7. do sport
8. ride a bike
9. go swimming
10. go to bed early

**Now do the quiz to find out if
you have a healthy lifestyle.
Circle the correct number.
Add up the points you circled and
find out your total score. Read the
analysis. Do you agree with it?
Why? / Why not?**

How often do you ...?

	Never	Sometimes	Every day
A. eat fruit and vegetables	0	1	2
B.	3	2	1
C.	0	1	2
D.	0	1	2
E.	3	1	0
F.	0	1	2
G.	2	1	0
H.	0	1	2
I.	2	1	0
J.	0	1	2

Analysis

18 or more: You are a very healthy person. You like to keep fit and you want to live a long life.

12–17: You want to be healthy and fit, but you like food that isn't good for you, and are sometimes a bit lazy.

6–11: You need to take your diet and exercise more seriously.

5 and under: You are very lazy! You don't care about what you eat or do to keep fit and healthy. Be careful!
Change your lifestyle before it is too late!

Choose a Job!

Look at the jobs in the box. Match them with the correct picture and write them on the lines. To find your ideal job, choose your best subject at school, answer the questions and follow the arrows.

translator
accountant
editor
tour guide
actor
sports teacher
marine biologist
newspaper reporter
physiotherapist
~~maths teacher~~
town planner
doctor
film director
farmer

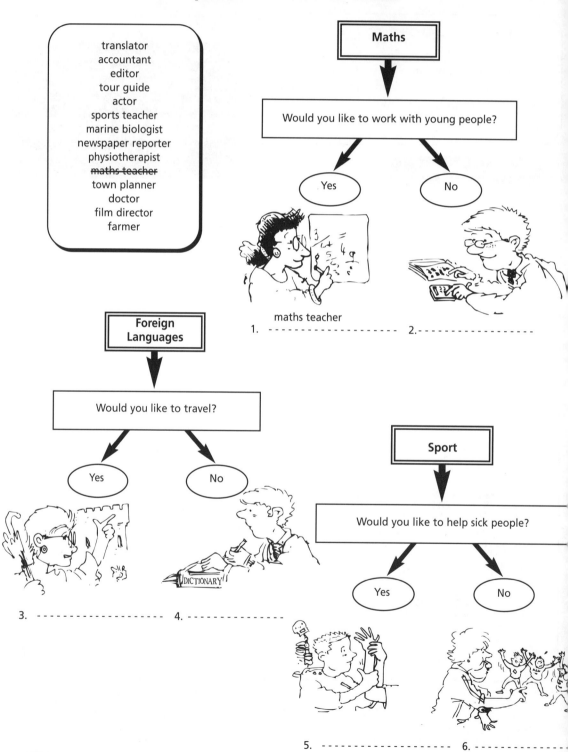

Maths

Would you like to work with young people?

Yes　　　　No

maths teacher
1. - - - - - - - - - - - - - - - - - - -　2. - - - - - - - - - - - - - - - -

Foreign Languages

Would you like to travel?

Yes　　　　No

3. - - - - - - - - - - - - - - - - - - -　4. - - - - - - - - - - - - - -

Sport

Would you like to help sick people?

Yes　　　　No

5. - - - - - - - - - - - - - - - - - - -　6. - - - - - - - - - -

Science

↓

Would you like to work with animals?

Yes   No

Literature

↓

Would you like to work in an office?

Yes   No

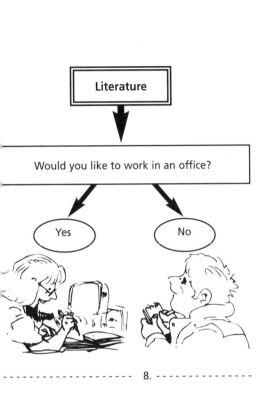

9. - 10. - - - - - - - - - - - - - -

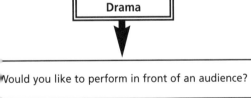

- - - - - - - - - - - - - - - - - - - 8. - - - - - - - - - - - - - - - -

Geography

↓

Would you like to work outside?

Yes   No

Music and Drama

↓

Would you like to perform in front of an audience?

Yes   No

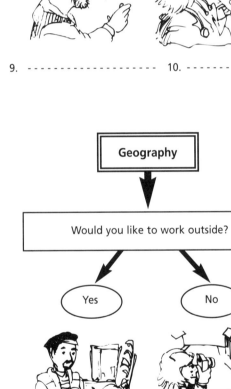

13. - 14. - - - - - - - - - - - - - - -

Which jobs suits you and why?

- - - - - - - - - - - - - - - - - - - 12. - - - - - - - - - - - - -

Who Lives Where?

Read the information and write the names.

Adam's home is at the end of the street. He lives on the fourth floor.

Danielle lives in a cottage, next door to Joe.

Jill lives in a mobile home, opposite Danielle.

Oliver lives in a flat, next door to Lisa and opposite Adam.

Michelle lives in a bungalow next door to the mobile home.

Mark lives in a large, modern house next door to Adam and opposite Lisa.

① _____

② _____

③ _____

④ _____

⑤ _____

⑥ _____

⑦ _____

⑧ _____

Mystery Objects

Look at the mystery objects. What are they? Circle a, b or c.

①
a. cooker

b. fridge

c. washing machine

②
a. toaster

b. tin opener

c. food mixer

③
a. sink

b. washing machine

c. microwave oven

④
a. dustpan

b. bowl

c. saucepan

⑤
a. vacuum cleaner

b. dustpan

c. broom

⑥
a. kettle

b. teapot

c. tap

How many of the kitchen objects mentioned in the exercise above can you find in this picture?

Picture Crossword

Complete the crossword.

Down

1

2

3

5

10

11

Across

4

6

7

8

9

12

13

Find the Bag!

The teachers have lost their bags!
Match the teachers with the bags.
Example: a) Geography

English

French

Biology

Technology

History

General science

Geography

IT (Information Technology)

PE (Physical Education)

Maths

Art

RE (Religious Education)

Choose the best name for each teacher.
Use a dictionary if necessary.

Examples:
Ms Belief – RE
Mr Metal – Technology
Mr Leaf – Biology

Mr Cambridge

Mr Numbers

Ms Croissant

Ms Portrait

Mr Metal

Ms X-ray

Mr Globe

Ms Past

Mr Leaf

Ms Belief

Mr Keyboard

Ms Marathon

School Timetable

Read the clues and complete Kieran's timetable.

• Kieran's favourite subjects are technology and science.

• He's got a double lesson of one of his favourite subjects on Friday.

• He's always got English in lesson 4 except Wednesday and Thursday.

• He's got one of his favourite subjects on Monday lesson 1 and Thursday lesson 3 after French and before history.

• On Monday, he's got IT and then PE.

• He's got one lesson of RE a week, on Tuesday after history and before English.

• He's got three maths lessons – on Tuesday, on Wednesday after art and on Thursday.

• He's got French on Thursday and on Friday after technology.

• He's got science on Thursday, after French.

• Wednesday starts with a double lesson and finishes with PE.

• He's got two science lessons each week.

	Monday	Tuesday	Wednesday	Thursday	Friday
lesson 1					
lesson 2					
lesson 3					
lesson 4					

Look at Kieran's schoolbag. What day is it?

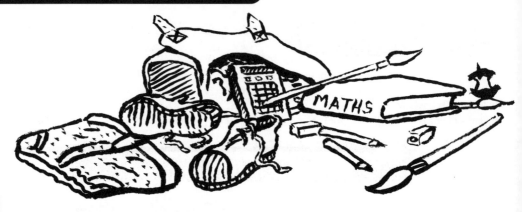

Back to School!

Complete the crossword. What did Kevin forget to buy?

**Make a list of the things that you need for school.
Are they the same as Kevin's things?**

School Tour

You are visiting a new school.

Playground

Answers

Page 4
My Family
1 brother 2 grandmother 3 uncle 4 mother 5 father 6 grandfather
7 aunt 8 sister

Emily is saying 'This is Andrew. He's my *cousin*.'

Page 5
Family Tree

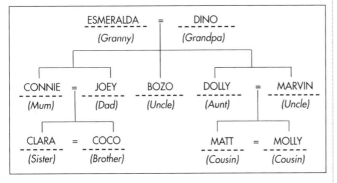

Molly is wrong. She's got *one* brother and two cousins.

Page 6
Football Training

The referee is tall. He's got short, dark hair. He doesn't wear glasses.

Page 7
The Monster
1 head 2 eye 3 chin 4 arm 5 hand 6 leg 7 foot
8 stomach 9 mouth 10 nose 11 ear

1 True 2 False. He's got four ears. 3 True 4 True
5 False. He's got one chin.

Page 8
Personality Spiral

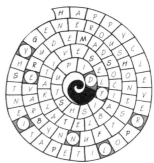

The alien is saying, 'I'm *friendly*.'

1 happy 2 generous 3 patient
4 brave 5 rude

Page 10
How Old Are You?
a True b True c False d True
e False f True g True h False
I True j True k False l True
m True n True o False p True

Lauren's cat is *10*.

Page 11
Inventions
1A 2M 3E 4R 5I 6C
7A 8N
The first jukeboxes were *American*.

Page 12
Puzzle It Out!
1 Simon 2 Carly 3 Anna
4 Robbie 5 Elena 6 Daniel
Luke feels *scared*.

Page 13
Feeling Ill
1 sore throat 2 cold
3 headache 4 toothache
5 stomach ache 6 earache
7 cut
The doctor says, *'Go to bed!'*

Page 14
In My Opinion
1 Fishing is boring. 2 Fishing is relaxing. 3 Parachuting is frightening. 4 Parachuting is exciting. 5 Shopping is irritating. 6 Shopping is great fun. 7 Reading is interesting.
8 Reading is OK.

Page 15
Dates for you Calendar
Ranjit's birthday – 3rd August
Christmas Day – 25th December
Bonfire Night – 5th November
Diwali – October
New Year's Day – 1st January
Valentines' Day – 14th February
Exams start – 10th May
Summer holidays start – 24th July
Mother's Day – March
Father's Day – June

Page 16
Numbers Picture
3 monkeys 2 elephants 4 lions
12 birds 5 sea lions 8 clouds
7 dustbins 14 children
3 zoo-keepers 10 trees
15 butterflies

Page 17
On the Washing Line
1 shirt 2 T-shirt 3 sweatshirt
4 skirt 5 jeans 6 trousers
7 dress 8 socks
Kevin is wearing *trainers*.

Page 18
Hide and Seek
Peter and Sophie

Page 19
Eurocolours
a Austria b Belgium
c Denmark d Finland e France
f Germany g Greece h Ireland
i Italy j Luxembourg
k Netherlands l Portugal
m Spain n Sweden
o United Kingdom

Page 20
Fruity Fun
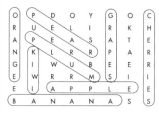

The worm's question is *Do you like strawberries?*

Page 21
Picnic Crossword

Nicky forgot *chocolate cake.*

Page 22
Which shop?
A BUTCHER'S B BAKER'S
C CHEMIST'S D NEWSAGENT'S
E PET SHOP F MUSIC SHOP
1 pet shop 2 newsagent's
3 chemist's 4 butcher's
5 music shop 6 baker's

Page 23
Health Quiz
1a 2h 3g 4e 5i 6b 7j
8c 9d 10f

Pages 24 and 25
Choose a Job
1 maths teacher 2 accountant
3 tour guide 4 translator
5 physiotherapist 6 sports teacher 7 editor 8 newspaper reporter 9 marine biologist
10 doctor 11 actor
12 film director 13 farmer
14 town planner

Page 26
Who Lives Where?
1 Jill 2 Michelle 3 Lisa
4 Oliver 5 Danielle 6 Joe
7 Mark 8 Adam

Page 27
Mystery Objects
1a 2b 3b 4c 5c 6a
Eight objects are in the picture – a teapot, a tap, a broom, a washing machine, a cooker, a kettle, a vacuum cleaner, a tin opener

Page 28
Picture Crossword

Page 29
Find the Bag!
a geography b art c maths
d technology e French

f science g biology h IT i RE
j English k PE l history

Suggested answers:
Mr Keyboard – IT
Mrs Marathon – PE Mr Globe –
geography Ms Portrait – art
Mr Numbers – maths
Mr Past – history Mr Metal –
technology Ms Croissant –
French Ms X-ray – science
Mr Cambridge – English

Page 30
School Timetable

	Monday	Tuesday	Wednesday	Thursday	Friday
1	science	maths	art	maths	technology
2	IT	history	art	French	technology
3	PE	RE	maths	science	French
4	English	English	PE	history	English

Page 31
Back to School!

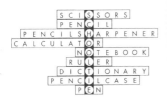

Pages 32 and 33
School Tour
1 reception   2 medical room
3 headteacher's office
13 staffroom   12 computer room
11 library   4 gym   5 assembly
hall   10 canteen   9 music room
8 language laboratory
The rooms that the students
don't visit are:
6 science laboratory
7 art room

Page 34
Football Facts
1D 2A 3V 4I 5D 6B 7E
8C 9K 10H 11A 12M
The famous English footballer is
David Beckham.

Page 35
Cine-madness!
1f 2b 3h 4a 5g 6d 7c 8j
9e 10i

Page 36
In the Department Store
1i 2f 3a 4e 5h 6d 7g 8c
9b 10j

Page 37
Find It!
1 steps   3 a clock   5 a chair
6 goggles   7 a whistle
9 armbands   10 a life guard
12 a swimming cap
14 a swimsuit   20 a diving
board

It's a *duck.*

Page 38
Translate!
1 bill   2 petrol   3 trousers
4 holiday   5 pavement
6 biscuit   7 dustbin   8 films
9 sweets   10 curtains
a10 b1 c9 d7 e3 f8 g5
h6 i2 j4

Page 39
Spot the Country!
France Italy Spain Greece
Austria Norway Sweden
Ireland Hungary Turkey

Pages 40 and 41
Crossword

Page 42
Transport Puzzle
The mystery from of transport
is **hovercraft**.

Page 43
Transport Quiz
1b   2b   3a, b, d, f   4b, f
1e   2d   3b   4a   5c

Page 44
At the Airport
1 FOREIGN CURRENCY
2 INFORMATION   3 TOILETS
4 DEPARTURE GATES
5 CHECK-IN   6 LIFTS
7 PASSPORT CONTROL
8 ARRIVALS   9 LEFT LUGGAGE

The passenger is saying,
'I MISSED MY PLANE!'

Page 45
Which Inventions?
A firework b skateboard
c internet d lawn mower
e hovercraft f dishwasher
1 lawn mower   2 hovercraft
3 dishwasher   4 skateboard
5 internet   6 firework

Page 46
What's the Weather Like?
Today it's *raining.*

1 raining; rainbow
2 cold; snowing   3 windy
4 cloudy; grey

Page 47
Environmental Quiz
1 200 litres   2 50 litres   3 1985
4 Between 18 and 48 kilometres
5 Because they contain CFC gas.
6 75   7 45 kilos   8 450 million
9 Unleaded petrol   10 Friends
of the Earth

The name of the organisation is *Greenpeace*.

Page 48
Summer Camp
1 surfing   2 canoeing   3 dancing   4 windsurfing   5 football   6 rock climbing   7 fishing   8 judo   9 volleyball   10 quizzes   11 drama   12 watching videos   13 karaoke
The activities not in the picture are *fishing* and *football*.

Page 50
Spot the Sport!
1 ice hockey   2 football
3 rugby   4 ice skating
5 basketball   6 cricket
7 skiing   8 judo   9 tennis
10 swimming   11 golf
The mystery sport is *horse-riding*.

Page 51
Sports Collocations
do: aerobics, gymnastics, taekwondo, yoga
go: jogging, skiing, horse-riding
play: snooker, baseball, volleyball, table tennis, hockey

Page 52
What Are You Watching?
1 cartoon   2 children's show
3 news   4 film   5 documentary
6 series   7 sports programme
8 talk show   9 gameshow

Page 53
Crazy Party!
A7   B1   C10   D9   E4   F5   G3
H2   I8   J6

Page 54
Musical Instruments
1 violin   2 recorder   3 cello

4 harp   5 flute   6 drums
7 trumpet   8 clarinet   9 piano
In an *orchestra*.

Page 55
In the Pet Shop
1j – tortoise   2i – snake
3g – rabbit   4c – hamster
5b – guinea pig   6e – parrot
7f – puppy   8d – kitten
9a – canary   10h – goldfish

Page 56
Pairs
1 horse   2 turkey   3 donkey
4 sheep   5 bull   6 piglet
7 chicken   8 cockerel   9 rabbit
10 goose   11 duck   12 goat
13 lamb

Page 57
Anna's Diary

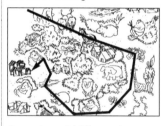

Anna stays at *Village A*.

Page 58
Animal Facts
1 true   2 false: elephant   3 true
4 false: cheetah   5 true   6 true
7 false: ostrich   8 true   9 true
10 false: koala   11 false
12 false: desert locust   13 true
14 false: Siberian tiger
The *cat* was the most sacred animal.

Page 59
Christmas Cards
1 mince pies   2 decorations
3 Christmas pudding   4 roast turkey   5 Christmas cake
6 card   7 cracker   8 Christmas

carol   9 Christmas tree
10 angel   11 bell   12 mistletoe
13 Father Christmas
14 chimney   15 present
16 reindeer   17 three kings
18 crib   19 star   20 snow

Page 60
Christmas Presents
1 trainers – Joe   2 video – Toby
3 chocolates – Chris   4 football – Rob   5 perfume – Sylvie
6 computer game – Mark
7 book – Julia   8 necklace – Lucy   9 board game – Mike
10 CD – Paul   11 jumper – Emma   12 sports bag – Nick

Page 61
Greetings!
1C   2F   3A   4E   5B   6D
1 Congratulations!   2 Happy Father's Day!   3 Good luck!
4 Goodbye!/Good luck!

Page 62
Holiday Souvenirs
a sunglasses   b postcard
c teddy bear   d flip-flops
e straw hat   f tea towel
g pencil case   h swimsuit
i necklace   j beach bag
k coffee mug   l T-shirt   m fridge magnet   n guide book
1 £14.75   2 £16.05   3 £11.40

Page 63
Holiday Code
1G   2A   3S   4V   5B   6M   7N
8P   9U   10T   11O   12L   13I
14E   15C
Tom went to *Scotland*.
Postcard A.

Read the text and follow the guided tour. Draw the route.

Welcome to Cherwell High School. The tour starts in the **playground**. Here is the school **reception**, you can come here for help and information ... and this is the **medical room**, where we send you if you are hurt or ill. Now we come to **headteacher's office** - she's called Mrs Stone. This is the **staffroom**, where the teachers sit and rest. And this room here is the **computer room**. Now we cross the corridor to the **library**. Here you can borrow books and videos ... And this is the **gym**, where we do sports. Next to it, over here, is the **assembly hall**, where all the students meet every Monday morning. This is the **canteen**, where we have lunch. This is the **music room** and finally, opposite the music room is the **language laboratory**.

Now label the rooms that you saw on your tour.

1. reception _____
○ _____
○ _____
○ _____
○ _____
○ _____
○ _____
○ _____
○ _____
○ _____
○ _____

Do you know the names of the rooms that you didn't visit?

○ _____
○ _____

Football Facts

How much do you know about football?
Read the sentences and choose the correct answers.

1. Who blows the whistle at the start of a match?
   the referee   D ...
   the linesman   M ...

2. What is the 15-minute break in the middle of the game?
   half-time   A ...
   extra-time   I ...

3. If a player commits a foul, he/she gets
   a goal   C ...
   a yellow card V ...

4. If the score is 0–0, it's called
   a draw   I ...
   a shoot-out   H ...

5. When a player moves the ball with his/her head, it's called
   a header   D ...
   a tackle   A ...

6. Football rules are
   different in each country   W ...
   international   B ...

7. In a team, there are
   11 players and 4 substitutes   E ...
   9 players and 6 substitutes   L ...

8. Football was invented
   in England   C ...
   in France   O ...

9. The first footballs were made of
   plastic   L ...
   leather   K ...

10. A football match for under-13s lasts
    70 minutes   H ...
    90 minutes   O ...

11. Goalkeepers wear
    shinpads   A ...
    helmets   S ...

12. A football top is called
    a blouse   T ...
    a shirt   M ...

What's your score?

Correct answers:

0–4
You aren't a football expert.

5–8
You're a keen football supporter.

9–12
You're football crazy!

Write the letters of the correct answers to spell the name of a famous English footballer.

The famous English footballer is

D _ _ _ _   _ _ _ _ _ _ _

Cine-madness!

Match the conversations to the people.

a. Excuse me, where are the toilets?
b. I'd like some popcorn, please.
c. Which screen is it for Star Wars?
d. One seat for Star Wars, please.
e. Mum, can we watch Blood Monster?

f. *Regular or large?*
g. *I'm sorry, it's sold out.*
h. In the foyer, next to the box office
i. *No, it's a certificate 18.*
J. Screen number 2

In the Department Store

What is everyone saying? Find the correct words for each person.

a. ~~Can I help you?~~

b. Can I try this on, please?

c. It's too big.

d. It's too expensive.

e. Do you sell football boots?

f. How much is the black one?

g. Keep the receipt in case you want to change it.

h. It's too small.

i. Can I pay by credit card?

j. The changing room is over there, on the left.

Find it!

Tick the things that are in the picture.

1. ✓   steps
2. ☐   a door
3. ☐   a clock
4. ☐   a window
5. ☐   a chair
6. ☐   goggles
7. ☐   a whistle
8. ☐   insects
9. ☐   armbands
10. ☐   a lifeguard
11. ☐   showers
12. ☐   a swimming cap
13. ☐   a boat
14. ☐   a swimsuit
15. ☐   a fish
16. ☐   sand
17. ☐   a pair of sunglasses
18. ☐   a ball
19. ☐   a bag
20. ☐   a diving board
21. ☐   a duck

What's this?

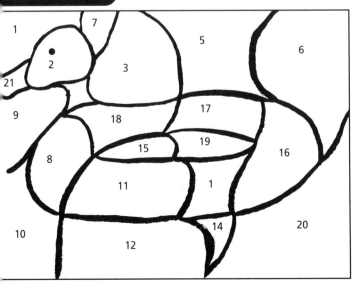

Colour the numbers that you ticked. Find one of the things on the list above.

It's a _ _ _ _ .

37

Translate!

Can you understand American English?
Find the English equivalents for these American words.

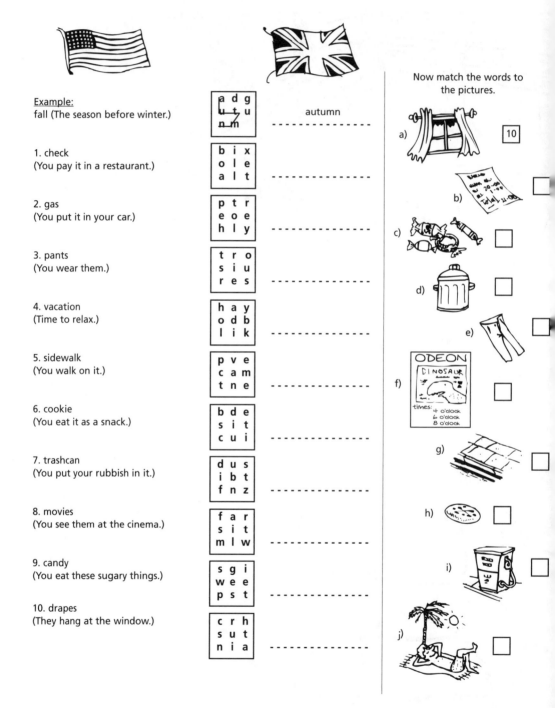

Now match the words to the pictures.

Example:
fall (The season before winter.)

a d g
u t u
n m

autumn
----

a)   10

1. check
(You pay it in a restaurant.)

b i x
o l e
a l t
----

b)

2. gas
(You put it in your car.)

p t r
e o e
h l y
----

c)

3. pants
(You wear them.)

t r o
s i u
r e s
----

d)

4. vacation
(Time to relax.)

h a y
o d b
l i k
----

e)

5. sidewalk
(You walk on it.)

p v e
c a m
t n e
----

f)

ODEON
DINOSAUR

times: 4 o'clock
6 o'clock
8 o'clock

6. cookie
(You eat it as a snack.)

b d e
s i t
c u i
----

g)

7. trashcan
(You put your rubbish in it.)

d u s
i b t
f n z
----

h)

8. movies
(You see them at the cinema.)

f a r
s i t
m l w
----

i)

9. candy
(You eat these sugary things.)

s g i
w e e
p s t
----

j)

10. drapes
(They hang at the window.)

c r h
s u t
n i a

Spot the Country!

Find the second half of each label to show where the passengers are going.

Write the names of the countries below.

‒ ‒ ‒ ‒ ‒ ‒ ‒ ‒ ‒ ‒ ‒   ‒ ‒ ‒ ‒ ‒ ‒ ‒ ‒ ‒ ‒ ‒   ‒ ‒ ‒ ‒ ‒ ‒ ‒ ‒ ‒ ‒ ‒

‒ ‒ ‒ ‒ ‒ ‒ ‒ ‒ ‒ ‒ ‒   ‒ ‒ ‒ ‒ ‒ ‒ ‒ ‒ ‒ ‒ ‒   ‒ ‒ ‒ ‒ ‒ ‒ ‒ ‒ ‒ ‒ ‒

‒ ‒ ‒ ‒ ‒ ‒ ‒ ‒ ‒ ‒ ‒   ‒ ‒ ‒ ‒ ‒ ‒ ‒ ‒ ‒ ‒ ‒   ‒ ‒ ‒ ‒ ‒ ‒ ‒ ‒ ‒ ‒ ‒

‒ ‒ ‒ ‒ ‒ ‒ ‒ ‒ ‒ ‒ ‒

Crossword

Do the crossword.

Across

1 You can watch a play here.

2 You can find the mayor here (2 words).

3 Tourists sleep here.

4 If you need information about the town, go to the ___ office.

5 If you are lost, look at a ___ to find out where you are.

6 You can go here on Sunday to pray.

7 You can arrive at the town at the ___ station.

8 This building is like a large church.

9 You go to a restaurant to ___.

10 You go here to buy stamps. (2 words)

11 You can go to the open-air swimming pool when the weather is ____.

12 The bus or train terminates here.

13 There is a lot of money here.

14 To report a crime, go to the ____ station.

Down

15 You can have lunch or dinner here.

16 There are lots of these at the campsite.

17 You can catch a ___ at a bus stop.

18 A bridge goes over it.

19 If you lose your umbrella, go to the ___ property office.

20 You can buy fresh vegetables and meat here.

21 You can go here to relax or do a sport.

22 The ___ of the hotel is 1, Beach Street.

23 You can put up your tent here.

24 If you are ___, you are not far away.

25 Nurses and doctors work here.

26 You can sit ___ a bench in the park.

27 What's the address —- the hotel?

28 If you want to watch a film, go to the ___.

29 You can buy things here.

Transport Puzzle

What is the mystery form of transport?
Are the sentences true or false? Follow the arrows.
The letters spell the name of a form of transport.

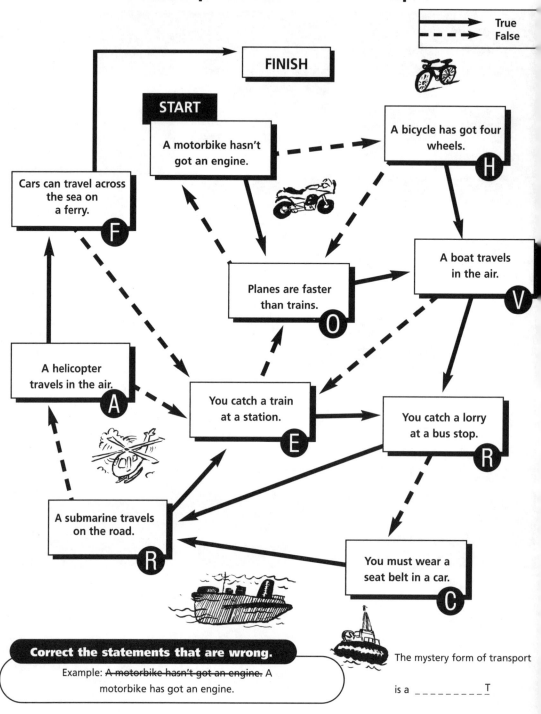

True
False

FINISH

START

A motorbike hasn't got an engine.

A bicycle has got four wheels.
H

Cars can travel across the sea on a ferry.
F

A boat travels in the air.
V

Planes are faster than trains.
O

A helicopter travels in the air.
A

You catch a train at a station.
E

You catch a lorry at a bus stop.
R

A submarine travels on the road.
R

You must wear a seat belt in a car.
C

Correct the statements that are wrong.

Example: ~~A motorbike hasn't got an engine.~~ A motorbike has got an engine.

The mystery form of transport

is a _ _ _ _ _ _ _ _ T

Transport Quiz

Choose the correct answers.

1. Which type of transport can you **get on** and **get off**?

a [ ] a car
b [ ] a train

2. Which type of transport can you **get in** and **get out of**?

a [ ] a motorbike
b [ ] a taxi

3 Which of these types of transport do you **catch**? There are four correct answers.

a [ ] a train   b [ ] a plane
c [ ] a bicycle   d [ ] a bus
e [ ] a car   f [ ] the underground

4 Which of these types of transport do you **ride**?
There are two correct answers.

a [ ] a ferry   b [ ] a scooter
c [ ] a coach   d [ ] a car
e [ ] a lorry   f [ ] a bicycle

atch the sentences with the pictures.

❶
Fasten your seatbelts – we're landing in five minutes.

❷
Welcome aboard! We sail from Portsmouth Harbour in thirty minutes.

❸
We're taking off! Here we go!

❹ Which stop do you want to get off at?

❺
Hyde Park? Get in! It's just around the corner.

At the Airport

What can you see at the airport?
Look at the signs and write the words.

1. | F | O | R | E | I | G | N | | C | U | R | R | E | N | C | Ⓨ |

2. | I | | | | | | Ⓞ | | | | |

3. | T | | | | | Ⓞ |

4. | D | | | | | | | | | | | | Ⓞ | |

5. | C | | | | | – | | Ⓞ |

6. | L | Ⓞ | | | |

7. | P | | | Ⓞ | | | | | | | | | |

8. | A | | | | | Ⓞ | |

9. | L | | | | | | | | Ⓞ | |

Now write the letters from inside the circles. What is the passenger saying?

—   — — — — — D
6   2   6   3   3   4

— —   — — — — — !
2   1   7   8   9   5   4

Which Inventions?

Match the two halves of each word to find six inventions.

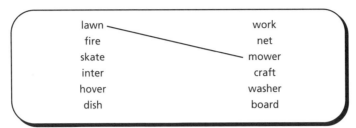

lawn	work
fire	net
skate	mower
inter	craft
hover	washer
dish	board

a)

_____

b)

_____

c)

_____

d)

_____

e)

_____

f)

_____

**Now read the descriptions.
Write the names of the inventions.**

1. You cut the grass with a lawn mower.

2. You can travel on water and land in a _____.

3. A _____ washes the dishes for you.

4. You stand on a _____ and it moves on its wheels.

5. You search the _____ with a computer.

6. A _____ explodes in the sky with a bang and colours.

What's the Weather Like?

Colour the weather words. What is the weather man saying?

Today it's _____

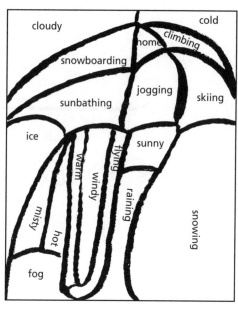

Look at the pictures and complete the sentences. Use the words in the box.

cloudy   cold   grey   raining
snowing   sunny   windy   rainbow

1 Today it's **sunny** but it's also _____.
Jack is looking at a _____.

3 Today it's fine and it's very _____.
Peter is flying his kite.

2 Today it's very _____.
It's _____.

4 It's _____ and the sky is _____.
Mrs Jones has got an umbrella.

Environmental Quiz

How much do you know about protecting the environment? Read these facts about protecting the environment and decide which are true and which are false. Circle your answer and put the letter in the box at the end. The letters will spell the name of an organisation concerned with protecting the environment.

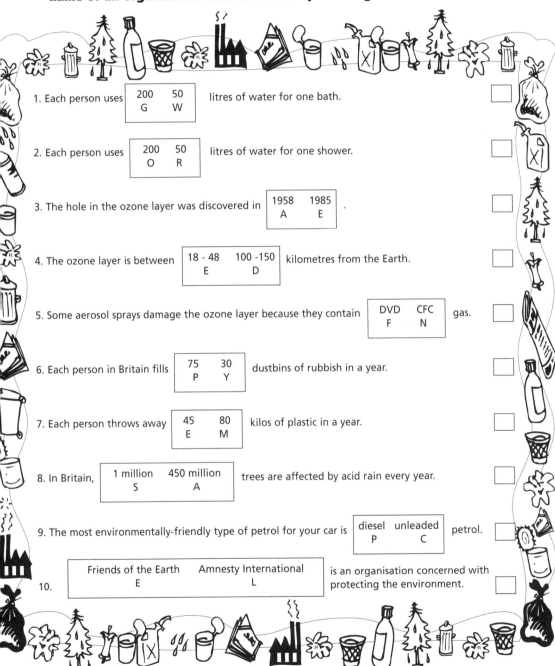

1. Each person uses | 200 (G) 50 (W) | litres of water for one bath. ☐

2. Each person uses | 200 (O) 50 (R) | litres of water for one shower. ☐

3. The hole in the ozone layer was discovered in | 1958 (A) 1985 (E) | . ☐

4. The ozone layer is between | 18 - 48 (E) 100 -150 (D) | kilometres from the Earth. ☐

5. Some aerosol sprays damage the ozone layer because they contain | DVD (F) CFC (N) | gas. ☐

6. Each person in Britain fills | 75 (P) 30 (Y) | dustbins of rubbish in a year. ☐

7. Each person throws away | 45 (E) 80 (M) | kilos of plastic in a year. ☐

8. In Britain, | 1 million (S) 450 million (A) | trees are affected by acid rain every year. ☐

9. The most environmentally-friendly type of petrol for your car is | diesel (P) unleaded (C) | petrol. ☐

10. | Friends of the Earth (E) Amnesty International (L) | is an organisation concerned with protecting the environment. ☐

Summer Camp

**Someone has rubbed all the vowels 'a, e , i, o, u' off the poster.
Write them back in to see the activities you can do at the camp.**

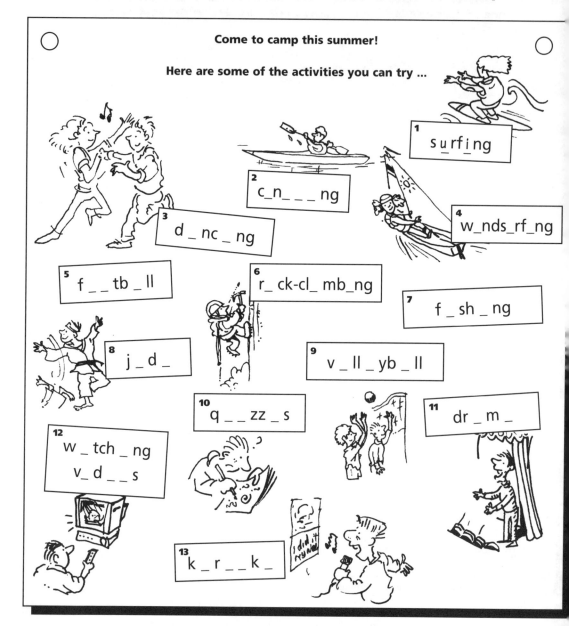

Come to camp this summer!

Here are some of the activities you can try ...

1 s u_ rf_ i ng

2 c_n_ _ _ ng

3 d _ nc _ ng

4 w_nds_rf_ng

5 f _ _ tb _ ll

6 r_ ck-cl_ mb_ng

7 f _ sh _ ng

8 j _ d _

9 v _ ll _ yb _ ll

10 q _ _ zz _ s

11 dr _ m _

12 w _ tch _ ng
    v _ d _ _ s

13 k _ r _ _ k _

**Two activities are not pictured on
the poster. Which?**

1. ....

2. ....

What's Your Ideal Holiday?

Do the quiz. Circle your answers.

1. You have nothing to do one sunny afternoon, so ...

★   you ask a friend to play a game of tennis.
▼   you go sunbathing.
✷   you start reading a new book.

2. Your best friend comes to your house, so ...

★   you go for a walk.
▼   you watch television.
✷   you play table tennis.

3. You are on your own at home, so ...

★   you play with a ball in the garden.
▼   you wash your hair.
✷   you surf the internet.

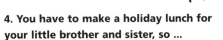

4. You have to make a holiday lunch for your little brother and sister, so ...

★   you cycle to a forest and have a picnic.
▼   you order some takeaways.
✷   you cook a Chinese meal.

5. For your holiday, you can only pack important things in your backpack, so ...

★   you take your swimming costume and snorkel so you can go swimming.
▼   you take your CD player and some CDs so you can listen to music.
✷   you take a pair of binoculars so you can go bird-watching.

6. What is your worst type of holiday?

★   Doing nothing and being bored.
▼   Rock climbing, canoeing, playing volleyball.
✷   Doing the same thing every day.

7. Which school trip would you choose?

★   Skiing in the mountains.
▼   Sunbathing at the beach.
✷   Sightseeing in London.

Count your symbols. How many have you got? Read the results.

Mostly ✷ You like to discover new things. Choose a holiday where you can visit new places.

Mostly ▼ You hate too much sport and activity. Choose a holiday where you can relax and be lazy.

Mostly ★ You love sport and activity. Choose a holiday where you can be active and make friends.

Spot the Sport!

Write the names of sports under the pictures. What is missing from each picture?

1

_ _ _ [ ] _ _ _ _

2

_ [ ] _ _ _ _ _

3

[ ] _ _ _ _

4

_ _ _ [ ] _ _ _ _ _

5

_ _ _ _ [ ] _ _ _ _

6

_ _ [ ] _ _ _ _ _

7

_ _ [ ] _ _ _

8

_ _ [ ] _

9

_ _ _ _ [ ] _

10

_ _ _ _ _ _ [ ] _

11

[ ] _ _ _

**Discover the mystery sport
with the letters in brackets.
What's missing from the picture?**

Mystery sport

_____

basketball

cricket

football

golf

ice hockey

ice skating

judo

rugby

skiing

swimming

tennis

What sports do you like?

Sports Collocations

Look at the list of sports, activities and leisure interests.
We use different verbs with different sports. Put the sports with the correct verb.

~~aerobics~~	hockey	skiing	taekwondo
baseball	horse-riding	snooker	volleyball
gymnastics	jogging	table tennis	yoga

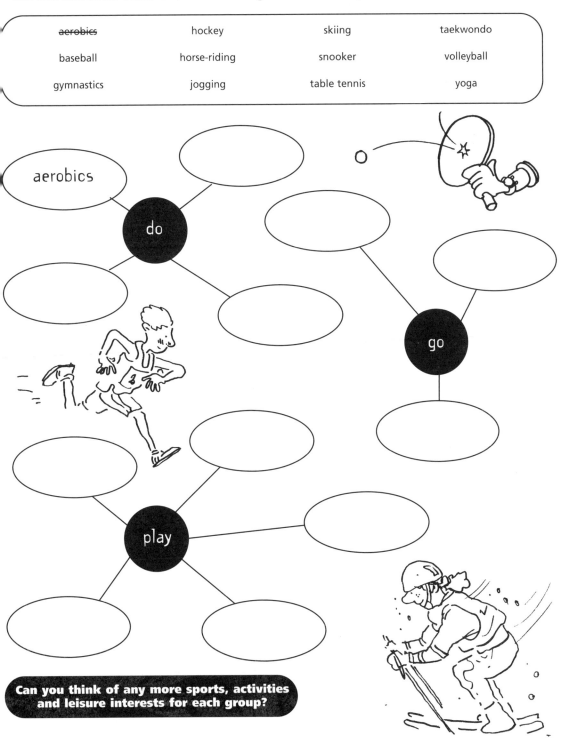

aerobics

do

go

play

Can you think of any more sports, activities and leisure interests for each group?

What Are You Watching?

Cross out the letters making up the title of each programme.
The letters remaining spell out what kind of programmes they are.
Write them under the televisions.

Sky 1

Locakrotomanon

1. _cartoon_

BBC Choice

Tcheilledren'stumsshow

2. _____

ITV

Ninghetlwyneşws

3. _____

Sky moviemax

Tfitainilmc

4. _____

Discovery

Wdoilcudlimenftarey

5. _____

Channel 4

Flasetrimaestes

6. _____

BBC 2

Mspoartchtsproofgrathemdamey

7. _____

Channel 5

O,taplkrshaow

8. _____

UK Gold

Gacomeunsthuopw

9. _____

What are your favourite television programmes?

Crazy Party!

Something's wrong! Find the correct bubble for each person!

A	B	C	D	E	F	G	H	I	J
7									

Musical Instruments

Unscramble the names of the musical instruments and write them in the grid.

❶ olivin

❷ creedror

❸ lolce

❹ raph

❺ tulfe

❻ smurd

❼ prumtet

❽ treclain

❾ anpoi

**Use the letters in the circles
to find the answer to this question.**

Where can you find all these
instruments together?

In an _____

In the Pet Shop

Can you match the words and pictures of the pets?

parrot   snake   rabbit
kitten   hamster   canary
puppy   guinea pig goldfish
           tortoise

A   B C D

F

E

G H I J

**Read the descriptions of the pets below their homes.
Then write the name of each pet in the correct homes.**

tortoise

1. I live in my shell. Touch it, and I'll go inside it!

2. I am long and thin, with scales on my shiny skin.

3. I like eating lettuce and carrots. Stroke my long ears!

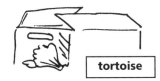

4. I am small and gold and furry, with tiny pink ears.

5. I am black and white and cuddly. You can't really see my ears!

6. I like talking! Look at my bright colours and big beak!

7. I like digging in the garden. Listen to my bark!

8. I like drinking milk. Feel my soft fur.

9. I can sing beautifully. Look at my lovely yellow feathers.

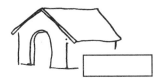

10. I am orange and I've got a tail. I don't make a noise.

**Which of these pets would you like?
Which wouldn't you like? Why?**

Pairs

Match the pieces of paper to find 13 farm animals.

Write the name of the animal under the correct picture.

1. <u>horse</u>

2. _ _ _ _ _ _ _ _ _ _

3. _ _ _ _ _ _ _ _ _ _

4. _ _ _ _ _ _ _ _ _ _

5. _ _ _ _ _ _ _ _ _ _

6. _ _ _ _ _ _ _ _ _ _

7. _ _ _ _ _ _ _ _ _ _

8. _ _ _ _ _ _ _ _ _ _

9. _ _ _ _ _ _ _ _ _ _

10. _ _ _ _ _ _ _ _ _ _

11. _ _ _ _ _ _ _ _

12. _ _ _ _ _ _ _ _ _

13. _ _ _ _ _ _ _ _ _ _

Anna's Diary

Anna is on safari. She passes lots of animals. Read her diary. Draw in her route. Where does she stop for the night (A, B, C or D)?

Today we saw an elephant, two lions, a zebra, three monkeys, a giraffe, two butterflies, a gorilla, a hippopotamus, an alligator, two tigers and another gorilla.

**Choose one of the other stopping-places.
Write a list of the animals you would see on your way there from the START.**

....

....

Animal Facts

What animal was most sacred to the ancient Egyptians?
To find out, read the sentences and choose TRUE or FALSE, then join the dots.
Example: If you think sentence 1 is true, join 2 and 50.
If you think it is false, join 2 and 27.
Use the internet to find out the facts.

		TRUE	FALSE
1.	The tallest animal is the giraffe.	2 - 50	2 - 27
2.	The animal with the longest nose is the dog.	27 - 50	27 - 5
3.	The largest animal is the blue whale.	5 - 16	5 - 13
4.	The fastest animal is the horse.	44 - 50	44 - 33
5.	The bird that is best at talking is the parrot.	39 - 3	39 - 16
6.	The most ferocious fish is the piranha.	46 - 50	46 - 31
7.	The largest bird's egg is laid by the eagle.	12 - 3	12 - 2
8.	The longest snake is the python.	13 - 27	13 - 50
9.	The loudest insect is the cicada.	36 - 46	31 - 13
10.	The fussiest eater is the rabbit.	16 - 18	16 - 44
11.	A hamster has eight eyes.	12 - 50	12 - 13
12.	The most destructive insect is the bee.	33 - 46	33 - 45
13.	The biggest lizard is the male komodo dragon.	10 - 36	10 - 12
14.	The largest member of the cat family is the wild cat.	3 - 27	3 - 45

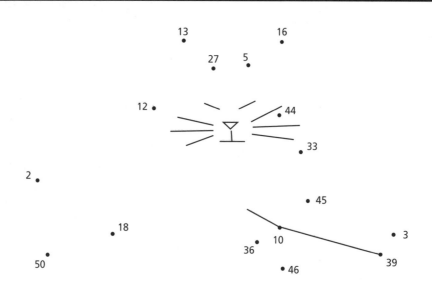

The .... was the most sacred animal to the ancient Egyptians.

Christmas Cards

Find the following objects on the Christmas cards.

Write the correct number next to each word.

angel	_ _	Christmas carol	_ _	decorations	_ _	reindeer	_ _
bell	_ _	Christmas pudding	_ _	Father Christmas	_ _	roast turkey	_ _
card	_ _	Christmas tree	_ _	mince pies	_ _	snow	_ _
chimney	_ _	cracker	_ _	mistletoe	_ _	star	_ _
Christmas cake	_ _	crib	_ _	present	_ _	three kings	_ _

Now join the dots in the same order as the list above. What object appears on the last Christmas card?

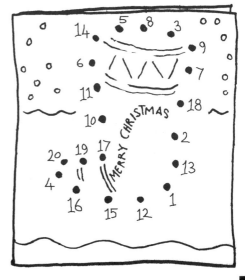

Christmas Presents

Help Father Christmas! Write what each present is.

trainers CD sports bag video perfume computer game
board game necklace football chocolates book jumper

⑧ n _ _ _ _ _ _ _

⑩ C _

① t r a i n e r s

⑥ c _ _ _ _ _ _ _ _ _ _

③ c _ _ _ _ _ _ _ _ _

⑨ b _ _ _ _ _ _

⑤ p _ _ _ _ _ _

⑦ b _ _ _

v _ _ _ _

②

④ f _ _ _ _ _ _ _

⑪ j _ _ _ _ _

⑫ s _ _ _ _ _ _ _ _ _

Now write the correct name on each label.

- Lucy loves jewellery.
- Nick is crazy about all sports.
- Jane likes designer clothes and shoes.
- Paul likes listening to music.
- Mike likes playing games.
- Emma likes new clothes.

- Julia reads a lot.
- Toby likes films.
- Rob loves football.
- Sylvie likes to smell nice.
- Chris loves chocolate.
- Mark's mad about computers.

Greetings!

Send each card on the right day! Match each card with the correct greeting.

1. Happy Birthday! ☐
2. Happy Mother's Day! ☐
3. Merry Christmas and Happy New Year! **A**
4. Congratulations! ☐
5. Good luck! ☐
6. Happy Valentine's Day! ☐

Write the greeting on each of these cards.

❶

❸

❷

❹

61

Holiday Souvenirs

Match the words to find the souvenirs.
Write them below the pictures.

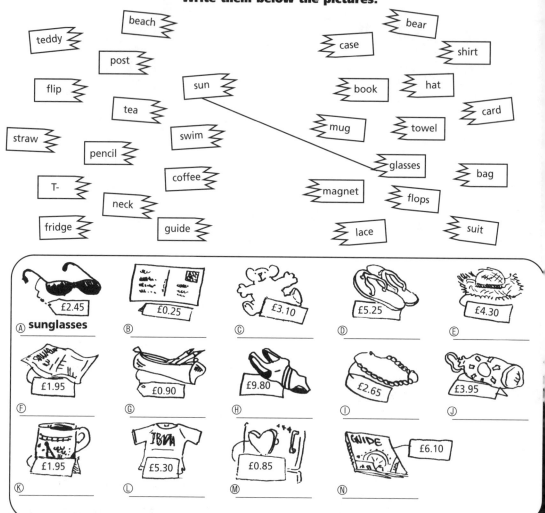

teddy

beach

post

bear

case

shirt

flip

sun

book

hat

tea

card

straw

swim

mug

towel

pencil

glasses

bag

coffee

T-

magnet

flops

neck

fridge

guide

lace

suit

£2.45
Ⓐ **sunglasses**

£0.25
Ⓑ

£3.10
Ⓒ

£5.25
Ⓓ

£4.30
Ⓔ

£1.95
Ⓕ

£0.90
Ⓖ

£9.80
Ⓗ

£2.65
Ⓘ

£3.95
Ⓙ

£1.95
Ⓚ

£5.30
Ⓛ

£0.85
Ⓜ

£6.10
Ⓝ

How much has each holiday-maker spent?

1 _ _ _ _ _ _ _ _ _ _ _ _ _   2 _ _ _ _ _ _ _ _ _ _ _ _   3 _ _ _ _ _ _ _ _ _ _ _

Holiday Code

Match the holiday verbs and nouns and write the code.

1. do	C swimming	1. = G
2. take	V a bicycle	2. =
3. buy	U a sandcastle	3. =
4. hire	A photos	4. =
5. eat	B an ice cream	5. =
6. visit	M a theme park	6. =
7. climb	N a mountain	7. =
8. board	G a bungy-jump	8. =
9. build	S souvenirs	9. =
10. make	T friends	10. =
11. watch	P the plane	11. =
12. send	O a musical	12. =
13. pack	L a postcard	13. =
14. play	I your suitcase	14. =
15. go	E beach volleyball	15. =

Use the code to read the holiday postcard.

Where did Tom go on holiday? Choose the correct postcard.

2-7-7-2,

_____

13 12-11-4-14 15-12-13-6-5-13-7-1 6-11-9-7-10-2-13-7-3

_____

5-9-10 5-14-7 7-14-4-13-3 13-3 10-11-11 5-13-1! 13 2-6

_____

4-13-3-13-10-13-7-1 6-9-3-14-9-6-3. 13 12-11-4-14

_____

12-13-3-10-14-7-13-7-1 10-11 5-2-1-8-13-8-14 6-9-3-13-15.

_____

12-11-4-14 10-11-6

_____

A SCOTLAND

B New york   MANHATTAN

C AUSTRALIA SYDNEY

Material written by: **Sue Finnie and Danièle Bourdais**

Commissioning Editor: **Emma Grisewood**

Content Editor: **Judith Greet**

Designers: **Tracey Mason (TM. Designs), Caroline Grimshaw**

Cover design: **Kaya-anne Cully**

Illustrations by: **Rachel Ball and Phil Burrows**

Mary Glasgow Magazines, an imprint of Scholastic Inc., 2003

Printed in the UK by Ashford Colour Press Ltd, Gosport, Hampshire